MW01113414

①

Once there was a beautiful, kind girl. Her stepmother made her do all the work, so her clothes were covered with dust and ashes. People called her Cinderella.

One day, her father came home with many presents. Instead of accepting anything precious, Cinderella only asked for a twig from a hazel tree.

Cinderella believed that hazel trees had spiritual qualities and so she planted the twig in front of her mother's grave.

Soon the twig grew into a big hazel tree. A white bird in it said to Cinderella, "I can help you and grant your wishes. Come and find me whenever you need me."

One day, Cinderella's stepmother told her two daughters that they were invited to a ball in the palace. "The king will choose a bride for his son," she said.

"May I go to the ball?" said Cinderella. "Look at your shabby dress! How can you go?" scoffed her stepmother. Then she and her daughters left for the ball.

Cinderella was very sad. She went to ask the hazel tree and the white bird for help. They granted her wish and gave her beautiful clothes and shoes.

After thanking the hazel tree and the white bird, Cinderella quickly put on the beautiful clothes and shoes and ran to the palace.

When Cinderella stepped into the ballroom her beauty stunned everyone. Indeed, the whole palace was brightened by her presence.

The prince asked Cinderella if she'd like to dance with him. Cinderella agreed happily. The prince said to her, "You are my favourite dance partner!"

The prince danced with Cinderella the whole evening, completely ignoring all the other girls. He really liked Cinderella and thought she was the right girl for him.

Cinderella left before the ball ended. The prince ran after her to see where she lived. Cinderella was in such a hurry that she dropped one of her shoes.

The prince quickly picked up the shoe and carried on running after Cinderella.

The prince followed Cinderella to her house, but he couldn't find her. He said to Cinderella's father, "I'll marry the girl whose foot fits into this shoe!"

The stepmother told her eldest daughter to try on the shoe. The girl tried so hard to squeeze her foot into the small shoe that she winced with pain.

Finally, she forced her foot in to the shoe. The prince kept his promise and lifted her onto his horse. She said goodbye to her mother and left with the prince.

As they passed the hazel tree, the white bird started to sing loudly, "The shoe doesn't fit, the shoe doesn't fit! She's not your queen, do not commit!"

Hearing this, the prince realised he had made a mistake and returned to the house. The stepmother called her second daughter to try the shoe.

The second daughter tried and tried and finally squeezed her big foot into the small shoe. Putting up with the pain, she got on the prince's horse.

When they passed the hazel tree, the white bird started singing again, "The shoe doesn't fit, the shoe doesn't fit! She's not your queen, do not commit!"

The prince returned to the house again. Cinderella's father said, "I have another daughter from my previous marriage. Why not ask her to try the shoe?"

Cinderella tried on the shoe. It was a perfect fit and, suddenly, the prince recognised her — she was the girl he had danced with the whole night at the ball!

As Cinderella and the prince rode past the hazel tree, the white bird sang, "The shoe's a good fit, the shoe's a good fit! She is your queen, be sure of it!"

Soon the prince and Cinderella were married. The white bird perched on Cinderella's shoulder singing a sweet song, and they all lived happily ever after.